Community of Scholars, Community of Teachers

Community of Scholars, Community of Teachers

Judith Shapiro

PRICKLY PARADIGM PRESS
CHICAGO

©2016 by Judith Shapiro.
All rights reserved.

Prickly Paradigm Press, LLC
5629 South University Avenue
Chicago, IL 60637

www.prickly-paradigm.com

ISBN: 9780984201099
LCCN: 2016946725

Printed in the United States of America on acid-free paper.

Prolegomenon: Hard Times

Not for the first time, and certainly not for the last, higher education in the United States is facing a number of serious problems (let us not euphemistically call them "challenges"). These need not be described in any detail here, since they are familiar and have been written about extensively: rising costs; escalating tuition; heavy student loan debt; government disinvestment; narrow-minded vocationalism, combined with the noxious strain of anti-intellectualism that regularly surfaces in our national discourse; the re-shaping of the professoriate as contingent academic labor grows in proportion to stable, full-time positions; governance struggles; confusion surrounding the uses and misuses of new information technologies; mission-diverting, out-of-control varsity athletics; pathologies of campus life that include ongoing ethnic/racial/religious divisiveness and a culture of sexual behavior that seems to range from the minimally rewarding to the outright criminal.

Above all, we see in the world of higher education the ever-growing savage inequalities of wealth that are increasingly defining our society more broadly. A stratum of well-endowed and highly sought after privileged institutions sit atop a financially pressed middle class of institutions and those that are struggling just to survive. This state of affairs is further aggravated by the fact that many of the institutions that serve the needs of their students most effectively and transformatively are in the bottom two groups.

As we work on many fronts to improve the general state of higher education, we can at least experience the positive reinforcement that comes with improving situations that are relatively under our control. And by "our," I mean those of us with the most direct control of what actually transpires in the process of higher education—that is to say, the faculty. This means taking a close, critical look at how and what we teach—at pedagogy, curricular content, and curricular coherence.

This involves adopting a comprehensive perspective on what is going on at different institutions, acknowledging and supporting the significant contributions of institutions located at various points up and down the academic food chain. Relatively wealthy, privileged institutions can learn much from casting their eyes below their usual sight lines. As it happens, students at some of the lesser-known small liberal arts colleges are getting a better education than students at some of our most high-profile universities. As it also happens, our society would be better served if the most dressed-for-success of our nation's college graduates were to benefit from just such an education.

Finally, at a time when we tend to focus on technological solutions to the problems we face, we might do well to turn our attention to something that is especially valuable for higher education, as it is for human life more generally: achieving strong, meaningful community.

I
I Do It My Way

A faculty member's classroom is, by tradition, his or her castle. Among the virtues of this tradition are that it serves academic freedom and leads to a special bond between a particular instructor and a particular group of students. A major disadvantage is that faculty members generally fail to benefit from their colleagues' experience and wisdom as teachers.

Academics would not think of pursuing research without being aware of what colleagues in the field were achieving in their work or benefiting from what their colleagues have learned from their failures (though there is less communication around the latter than would be useful). Why should faculty not profit similarly with respect to their teaching?

There are master teachers who seem to be naturals at the task. There are true eccentrics whose students appreciate them the way an oenophile would appreciate a rare wine. But such teachers are not found in abundance. And most faculty members—even the best—stand to benefit from working together to explore, experiment with, and evaluate approaches to teaching that lead to deeper and more enduring learning.

Faculty members profit, for example, from reviewing together what the field of cognitive science has shown about the relative effectiveness of particular presentation strategies and study habits. They have been led to consider how involving students in "meta" conversations about their own learning trajectories can have significant pedagogical advantages. Something as simple and apparently obvious as opening a syllabus with an outline of what students should be expected to know and to do as a result of taking a particular course can focus the student (and faculty) mind wonderfully. These are things we learn from talking about teaching with one another.

The higher education press is full of information on how some faculty members have worked together around these and other teaching-related matters. Such accounts are, however, too often written in the kind of professional jargon that is appealing only to the already-converted. The literature on higher education too often reflects a prose style that can be rebarbative even to those of us basically friendly to its content.

Some of its terms are worth adopting for their useful shorthand functions; at the same time, they can easily be rendered in traditionally recognizable language in the interests of outreach. "High impact practices" are styles of teaching that use class time to engage students actively—having them work in groups, solve problems together, engage in conversation with one another and with the instructor—as opposed to passively receiving information, which is something they can do on their own outside of class. The result is a "flipped classroom," meaning a reversal of the usual situation in which class time is a relatively passive experience for students as they sit listening to the professor lecture and take on more individual and active responsibility for their work outside of class hours; "flipping" involves having students come to class already prepared with the information-gathering side of their work, that does not require their co-presence in the classroom, while class time itself is reserved for the kinds of engaged, interactive learning that happen when people are together in one place. A brilliantly delivered lecture can itself be a high impact practice, bringing the audience together in communal appreciation, even awe; the problem is that such lectures are greatly outnumbered by those that fall short of this mark.

High impact practices and flipped classrooms lead to a less boring experience for both students and faculty members, which is not irrelevant to how much learning goes on. They also put on-line resources in their proper place with regard to the distinctive power of a residentially-based liberal arts educational experience: integrated intelligently into the overall work of the course. They contrast with a MOOCmania (the term MOOC being an acronym for Massive Open On-line Course) that too often focuses on the wide distribution of on-line lecture courses by famous faculty members—a project not all that different from a television show called "Sunrise Semester," which first aired in 1957 and featured New York University's Dr. Floyd Zulli (a program that some of us are old enough to remember).*

---

*As an aside—professional conferences would also benefit from attention to higher impact practices. How many of us have sat through scholarly papers read at a high rate of speed in order to

It has often been pointed out that high impact practices and greater curricular coherence are especially important for students who have been relatively ill-served—socioeconomically and educationally—in their pre-college years. Meeting their needs in a life-altering way has always been one of the higher goals in American higher education.

As it happens, however, students from privileged backgrounds are themselves not as prepared for college-level work as one might expect. A faculty member at one of the most elite liberal arts colleges in America who prepared a special program for relatively disadvantaged entering students soon found that his colleagues—faced with pervasive student deficits in such areas as writing, critical thinking, and effective research techniques—were interested in extending the program across the student body more widely.

Another benefit of conversation about teaching has to do with the fact that faculty are of different generations from one another, some closer in age to those in our classes. It can be useful to connect with the peer culture of our students, making immediately resonant connections and then moving on to less historically parochial territory. We do not need to go native, which serves neither their needs nor our own. Rather, we can think of ourselves as anthropologists, enjoying some necessary familiarity with the culture in

---

come in under the time limit (a goal too often not met), terminally bored and looking repeatedly at our watches. It is extraordinary how enduring this ritual has proven to be; it is even observed by sociolinguists who make it their business to study speech in social context. And it is not as if the professional conference low-impact-practice ritual is a colorful one—no incense, chanting, or elegant costumes, for example. Think of how much more interesting meetings could be if session organizers experimented with some of the varying formats being tried out in classrooms.

which we ply our trade. This should come naturally to us because of our own intellectual curiosity; at the same time, we can lead our students into the more informed, comparative stance of outsiders.

Coming together in an ongoing way to reflect on what our respective courses contribute to the over-all educational experience of our students makes their time with us more coherent. This differs from the intermittent curriculum reviews that too commonly descend into a log-rolling enterprise in which departments seek to defend their own interests in whatever package of general education requirements will be viewed as sufficiently harmless and open-ended to be approved by the faculty as a whole.

If working together benefits undergraduates, it is also crucial for the transformation of graduate student education. The belated realization that students planning a career in academia might profit from preparation for teaching as well as for research has too often led to an out-sourcing of such preparation to "centers" for teaching and learning; these might, in too many cases, better be termed "peripheries," given their level of detachment from the ongoing life of the departments in which faculty members spend their working lives. While such centers usually provide welcome and appropriate forms of professional peda-gogical expertise, what they require in order to realize their mission is a close, collegial connection to discipli-nary and interdisciplinary departments and to the faculty therein.

Changes along the lines I am advocating here are occurring with increasing frequency. Interestingly enough, they are least visible in our nation's most priv-ileged colleges and universities. This is not surprising, given where complacency is most likely to flourish and where, on the other hand, necessity may serve as the mother of invention. My own first faculty appointment in a very high altitude institution occurred decades ago and times have perhaps changed somewhat since the era when raising the subject of teaching in a conversation with a colleague would most definitely have been *infra dig*, the professional equivalent of a burp. Yet it seems that the privatization of teaching is still relatively the norm in such places. They will probably be among the last places where one's "work" (research) is seen in opposition to one's "load" (teaching).

The issues I am raising here are hardly new. There is an extensive literature on teaching and learning in higher education that has grown out of experiences faculty members have sought to share with their colleagues. We can go back, for example, to reports published in the 1980's about how science and mathematics could be taught more effectively and see how the same arguments still have to be made well into the second decade of the 21st century.

A mind is a terrible thing to change.

So, I write not with the goal of imparting new knowledge, but from the realization that Newcastle seems, oddly enough, to be short on coal. I also write from a sense of fellowship with those who have resisted the very kinds of change I am arguing for. To them—to you, to us—I say that we do not forgo the mysteries of our particular, individual connection to our students when we learn from one another how to serve them better. What brings traditionalists and innovators together is a love for teaching. In the beginning is the vocation.

II
Reacting to the Past: A Case Study

When I decided to return to teaching after 22 years as an academic administrator—first as a provost and then as a president—I decided that what I truly wanted to teach was *Reacting to the Past*, a course structured around intellectually sophisticated games set at various turning points in history. Developed by a member of the Barnard College faculty, *Reacting to the Past* has since spread to over 300 colleges and universities in the United States and has more recently extended its reach abroad.

  Reacting to the Past classes basically work as follows: The instructor spends a couple of sessions providing background to the period, events, and reading materials to be used in the game. Most of the students in the class are then divided into factions that pursue their own mutually conflicting interests. Students not assigned to factions are known as "indeterminates" and have an important role in deciding which faction will win.

In the first *Reacting* game to be developed, which takes place in Athens in 403 B.C. at the conclusion of the Peloponnesian War, the factions are Radical Democrats, Moderate Democrats, Oligarchs, and Socratics. Radical Democrats seek a broadly-based electorate, leaders drawn by lots, restoration of the Athenian Empire, and the silencing of Socrates. Moderate Democrats share many of these goals, but are more apt to compromise. Oligarchs are united in their contempt for democracy as a mode of government and distrustful of imperial adventures. Socratics believe in government by an elite defined by wisdom as opposed to wealth.

Indeterminates in the game have their own individually distinctive identities and goals: one is a rich athlete who dreams of becoming an absolute ruler of Athens in the mold of Alcibiades; another is an impoverished farmer who stands to benefit if citizens are paid for participating in the political life of the Assembly and if a restoration of Athenian military dominance causes food prices to rise; yet another is a metic (foreigner) who seeks to gain the same rights as those born in Athens in order to balance his financial obligations as a resident. Some indeterminates are more open-minded than others who are already tending in their sympathies to one or another of the factions.

Originally, there was only one actual historical character in the Athens game: Thrasybulus, hero of the civil war victory against the Thirty Tyrants and their Spartan supporters, now leader of the Radical Democrats. Characters in this *Reacting* game as well as others have generally been fictional, though more recent versions of long-standing games, including this one, have been adding the number of historical figures.

The major issues to be decided in the course of the Athens game include the following: Should a reconciliation agreement be reached so that there are no lawsuits or other punishment against supporters of the Thirty Tyrants? Should property ownership be a requirement for voting? Should citizens be paid for attending Assembly sessions? Should metics be allowed to vote? Should the Athenian navy be restored and the long walls between the port of Piraeus and the city of Athens be rebuilt with funds raised by taxes? Should Socrates be tried and, if so, convicted?

Matters of consequence must be resolved in every *Reacting to the Past* game. In a game set in China during the declining years of the Ming Empire, a major issue is whether the Wanli Emperor should get to name as successor his second son by a favored concubine over his first son by his senior wife, a question tied to whose perspectives should dominate the Grand Secretariat of the Hanlin Academy in the Forbidden City—the voice of Confucian purists or that of their more practical-minded colleagues? In the Massachusetts Bay Colony of the 1630's, decisions must be made about which newly arrived immigrants should be admitted to membership in the Boston Church based on the narratives they give of their own conversions; this, in turn, will determine who is eligible to vote in the General Court when Anne Hutchinson is tried for sedition. Among the questions raised in France during the Revolution are: Is it justified to use violence to oppose oppression? Should the nation continue to have a king? If so, should that king have a veto over legislation? Should the legislature be bicameral or unicameral? Should a right to property be included in the formulation of the rights of man? Should the Civil Constitution of the Clergy stand or be revoked? Can Lafayette be trusted by the common people?

Reading materials for *Reacting* courses include a gamebook and various additional outside readings. Gamebooks open with a novelistic vignette that helps students to imagine themselves in the setting of the game. The introduction to imperial China comes in the person of a senior, distinguished Grand Secretary awakening from one of his recurrent nightmares about being unprepared for his first set of major examinations and thus being faced with dishonoring the many relatives who sacrificed so much for his success. The world of the Massachusetts Bay Colony opens first through the wandering eye of a young man seated in Church who is distracted from the pastor's fiery sermon on original sin by glimpses of a married woman in the congregation for whom he feels an obsessive desire; does this mean he is among the damned?

The gamebook then provides fuller historical background information for the game, including a list of concepts central to the culture of the period. Game instructions follow, including an outline of major episodes in the game and their various possible outcomes. Some descriptions are given of the various groups and *dramatis personae* involved in the game, but a significant amount of information is provided confidentially in special role sheets for factions and individuals. Secrecy, deal-making, and strategizing are all part of the game.

Appendices to the gamebook include various primary and secondary sources germane to the historical situation. Students are also assigned additional outside readings. In the Athens game, for example, students read Plato's *Republic*. In the China game, they read *The Analects* of Confucius.

Secondary sources, aside from allowing students to encounter contributions by distinguished scholars of the period, enable them to see how historians evaluate sources, interpret information, and engage in arguments about how to view the past. This experience is of particular value in helping them steer through the Scylla of naïve positivism and the Charybdis of anything-goes relativism—two clear and present dangers for undergraduates.

Reacting games can be counterfactual, but only within reason. Athenians cannot rebuild their imperial navy with submarines. Louis XIV and Marie-Antoinette cannot be rescued by helicopter during their flight to Varennes. On the other hand, Socrates may be found innocent and not have to drink hemlock. The French Revolution may be put down by a successful invasion of France led by royal allies in other countries.

Games are not necessarily fair—not all factions have an equal chance of winning. But, then again, neither is history—or life—fair. There are moments in a game when the outcome is determined by a roll of the dice. Chance has its part to play. The games are, however, structured such that all factions have strong incentives to seek interim triumphs and ultimate victory.

In post-game class sessions, instructors share information on the true historical record insofar as we know it, so that students will come away with shared knowledge about what actually happened. At the same time, students develop a sense of the role of contingency and human agency in history. Post-game sessions also provide an opportunity for students to reflect on the experience of playing the game, a useful exercise in self-examination and thinking about their own learning process.

In the course of a game, students have to take their best shot at various forms of discourse appropriate to the times. If they are Grand Secretaries in the

Hanlin Academy, their speeches to the Emperor must be in the form of decorous, allusive memorials. If a student is the Pastor of the Boston Church, that student will have to deliver compelling sermons. Most oral presentations need to be made without reading from a text, though notes may be referred to. And all sessions involve lively debates where students have to combine an ability to speak on their feet with the background knowledge needed to make their remarks substantive and persuasive.

Written assignments also conform to culturally and historically diverse patterns. Factions in the French Revolution game, for example, have to put out weekly newspapers that include reports of events, editorials, political cartoons and various other features that students come up with once their imaginations are stirred.

Students are responsible for both individual work and for the product of group effort. They are responsible not only to themselves and to the instructor, but also to one another.

Reacting games are an immersion into a different cultural world where students inevitably bring their own beliefs and interests with them even as they try to wrestle with situations and concepts that are truly foreign. They broaden their horizons not only through exotic encounters, but by gaining an ability to see their own world with more critical distance, an experience that has been analyzed in German writings as *Verfremdung* and in Russian ones as *ostranenie*— that is, defamiliarization.

Students bring not only their intellects, but also their emotions, their passions to their work, which makes for a highly engaging classroom experience. The competitive nature of the games is central to heightening the energy level. Students truly have their skins in the game.

And what of the part played by the faculty member once the class switches into game mode? He or she takes on the dual role of instructor and gamemaster, moving to the periphery of the classroom to observe, intervene discreetly to help from time to time (usually by passing notes to players), provide the intermittent punishments and rewards specified in the game, and, at some moments in some games, intervening in a ways that shape the outcome. The instructor/gamemaster may also have to get matters back on track if things get too far out of constructive bounds, though a certain amount of disorder is both useful pedagogically and accurate in terms of historical verisimilitude.

The creator of *Reacting to the Past*, Mark Carnes, is a distinguished historian of the United States whose research accomplishments are matched by a deep dedication to teaching. The story of how he came to develop this approach is described in his 2014 book *Minds on Fire*. To put it bluntly, as he does, he discovered that too many of his very bright, high-achieving Barnard and Columbia students found most of their courses "kinda boring."

A *Reacting* class, on the other hand, is never boring, especially since it sometimes looks as if it is going off the rails—not unlike the events portrayed. Faculty members report that students attend without fail, except in cases of illness or family emergency. The activities in which students engage are those "high impact practices" mentioned earlier, though Carnes was there *avant la lettre*.

It is notable that Carnes, possessed of a strong liberal arts education himself, began by developing

Reacting games well beyond his own scholarly specializations. His original games have grown in sophistication as they have attracted collaborators and gamebook co-authors who are scholars of those different times and other places. New games have continued to emerge as faculty members decide to use *Reacting* pedagogy for their own fields. And so, we have games that focus on struggles between Henry VIII and the Reformation Parliament; on the trial of Galileo, pitting the "new cosmology" against the authority of the Catholic Church; on debates in the Royal Society of London about awarding the Copley Medal to Charles Darwin; on political ferment in Greenwich Village in 1913 as suffragists and labor organizers compete for support and attention; on India in 1945 as the British prepare to depart; on South Africa in 1993 after Nelson Mandela has emerged from prison and Apartheid is collapsing.

Faculty members have shown a special interest in developing games in their own areas of research specialization. At the same time, it is important that they continue to find value in teaching beyond those narrower interests if there is going to be a counter balance to the centrifugal forces that are making college curricula increasingly fragmented. Teaching beyond one's comfort zone enables a faculty member to learn along with the students. And, surely, it should be possible to keep sufficiently ahead of a group of undergraduates in order to justify being the one that gets paid as opposed to the ones paying.

Reacting to the Past has been adopted at a wide range of institutions from liberal arts colleges to large public universities to community colleges. It can be played with classes of various sizes, though many consider the ideal class size to be between 18 and 25.

Workshops provide the major vehicle for dissemination, game development, and ongoing experimentation. Participants play abbreviated versions of games and also attend discussion sessions on a variety of curricular and pedagogical matters. Veterans mingle with newcomers interested in exploring the program. Participants remain in touch through various on-line vehicles, where they can share resources, seek advice, and answer one another's questions.

Reacting to the Past is a paradigm case of what is possible when faculty members form a community of teachers. It has attracted participants at various stages in their careers—from junior faculty in the early years of their appointments to senior faculty who have found it a source of professional and intellectual revitalization. It enables faculty members to share with their students not only their commitment to a particular field of scholarship or science, but also their common commitment to a broad, deep, rich, and rewarding liberal arts education.

For further information on *Reacting to the Past*, see *Minds on Fire* by Mark Carnes (Harvard University Press, 2014) and visit the *Reacting* website at www.barnard.edu/reacting

III
That's Not My Department

Once the rockets are up
Who cares where they come down.
"That's not my department,"
Says Werner Von Braun.

—Tom Lehrer

Faculty members tend to live in their disciplinary departments. This is understandable, given their attachment to their fields, their graduate students (for those who have them), and their majors. And yet, they have wider responsibilities, especially if they are fortunate enough to belong to those faculty ranks with relative job security who can reasonably expect a long-term future in the academy.

For openers, they might expand their thinking about the goals of their own departments. And, then, they might devote more energy to expanding their focus to the more general mission of the institutions of which they are a part (and which, by the way, pay their salaries).

So, first, are faculty members taking an overly provincial approach, both intellectually and professionally, to their respective departmental programs? It has been pointed out that, insofar as an undergraduate major is focused on what a student will need to enter a graduate program, it is more properly seen as vocational training than as an integral part of a liberal arts education. Majors with relatively heavy requirements lead to a level of specialization that may be desirable for some students, but unnecessary and premature for others. They are also an obstacle to the serendipitous discovery and delight that can come from taking a course that falls into the residual category of "electives." It is always possible to serve the interests of those heading to graduate school in the field by providing special enhancements to the major.

Faculty members should also consider how the undergraduate departmental major can and should connect more organically with the wider curriculum of the institution. This interest is not served simply by creating new interdisciplinary programs, since too often these have simply resulted in a proliferation of department-like entities, as opposed to greater intellectual coherence in the undergraduate experience as a whole.

On occasions when faculty come together for the lengthy, intensive process of an institution-wide "curriculum review," the outcome too rarely justifies the time and energy expended. (I believe comparative research would show that, in general, the more elite the institution, the more modest the results.) Aside from their ritual dimension, such processes commonly involve a bargaining approach in which faculty members arrive at agreements about "general" or "distributional" requirements in terms of how their respective departmental interests are being served.

And yet, there have been some curriculum reviews that actually aim to make the student experience intellectually coherent, providing room for varying interests and passions while creating a student community that reflects the mission and identity of the institution. Some of us in the foundation world have been in a position to facilitate this process, supporting those who are doing the good work.[§]

Graduate programs might also better serve their students' interests. Leaving aside the question of preparing graduate students for careers outside the academy altogether, graduate programs need to consider preparing them for the range of institutions within the universe of higher education in which they may find themselves. This means focusing on preparing students as teachers and not just as researchers, especially since their students' chances of getting positions in research universities are clearly shrinking—though, even in such universities, better preparation as teachers would stand them in good stead.

Given that teaching assistantships are an important way of financially supporting graduate students, departmental faculty must decide whether they are viewing those students as junior colleagues or as cheap

---

[§]Some examples include the following multi-institutional initiatives: "Gateways to Liberal Education" (Ursinus, Rhodes, Lawrence, and Holy Cross); "Core Curricula in the Research University" (Columbia, Yale, University of Chicago) a project that has developed to involve members of the just-mentioned "Gateways" group; "The Senior Capstone: Transformative Experiences in the Liberal Arts" (Allegheny, Augustana, Washington, Wooster). Descriptions of these projects can be found on the Teagle Foundation website (www.teaglefoundation.org).

labor. This choice clearly influences how graduate students see themselves, as well as how well equipped they are for their working lives after graduation. Is responsibility for helping them develop as teachers being farmed out to teaching and learning centers, which—as noted already—are all too often peripheral to the life of departments? Or are there the strong collaborative ties between such centers and departmental faculty that are essential to the professional development of graduate students?

Some graduate programs are stepping up to this particular plate;[‡] more need to do so. Perhaps one way of getting their attention is to present them with the following choice: either (1) broaden the graduate program to properly prepare admitted students for a wider range of careers in higher education and beyond, or (2) limit the number of admitted students to those who are either likely to find jobs in research universities or who are interested in graduate education for its own sake and harbor no expectations about how the program will advance their future careers. Departments choosing the second option would have to find other ways for senior faculty members to occupy their time, which might possibly involve teaching undergraduates.

To put these two options in terms of reproductive biology: some species follow what is termed the r-selection strategy, in which a large number of offspring are produced and few are expected to survive. On the other hand, species that pursue the K-selection strategy produce fewer offspring, but invest in them heavily,

---

[‡]A 2016 report by Jo Beld and Tim Delmont provides a detailed review and evaluation of projects carried out at Stanford, Northwestern, Columbia, Princeton, Cornell, Berkeley, and the American Historical Association. The report is available at www.teaglefoundation.org.

which results in their relatively high survival rate. Graduate departments, being (generally) composed of human beings, should presumably follow the strategy characteristic of our species.

And if, to continue the biological metaphor, we take note that evolutionary theory in general has come to emphasize cooperation as well as competition, we want to be sure that academics, as a population, are not so focused on departmental rivalries and individual career ambitions that they fail to have a sufficient regard for the common good—the common good, in this case, being the kind of education we want to provide for our students.

Returning to the undergraduate curriculum, it may be useful to take a Hegelian perspective to recent trends and how best to view the path forward.

First, we had the *"thesis"*—that the curriculum was essentially a matter of its content. This was all the easier to believe when there could be general agreement about what an educated person should know. But as scholarship, science, and knowledge in general grew apace, it became less possible to agree on what this was. Centrifugal forces of various kinds led to curricular proliferation.

Given these forces, and also the fact that teaching and learning have also always been about the intellectual capacities developed thereby, we began to see a focus on what we might call "skills," "capacities," or "competencies." This we may consider the *"antithesis"* moment. To be sure, many of those who turned to a focus on "competencies" continued to care very much about content, but attention shifted away from it.

Clearly, a *synthesis* is called for in which the educated mind needs both an effective design and high-quality furniture. And this will only happen once we move beyond an all-too-common state of affairs that has been described in especially memorable terms by Robert Zemsky: "It is as if the way to run an upscale restaurant is to allow every customer to define his or her own menu and the chefs in the kitchen to cook only what they wanted to cook."[△]

An impressive case for what can be achieved when faculty work together to shape a curriculum can be seen in Yale-NUS College, a partnership created by Yale University and the National University of Singapore. Most of the attention given to this institution in the higher education press has focused on concerns about academic freedom when institutions establish partnerships or branches abroad. While this issue is not unimportant, Yale-NUS presents a sufficiently compelling example of curricular reform for its accomplishments to merit significant attention back here on the home front.

All undergraduates at Yale-NUS share a core curriculum that includes a common set of courses in the first two years. In year one, the themes are Literature and the Humanities, Philosophy and Political Thought, Scientific Inquiry, and Comparative Social Institutions. In year two, they include Modern Social Thought and a second science course; electives

---

[△]This particular wording was used in a personal communication, but the general point is made in a number of Zemsky's writings, including *Checklist for Change* (Rutgers University Press, 2013). The restaurant analogy is used to similar effect by P.F. Kluge, who is here thinking of the most basic prerequisites to a liberal education: "Hell of a menu at this Italian restaurant. Only—rescue me! —WE FORGOT THE KNIVES AND FORKS! WE DIDN'T SET THE TABLE! SOME OF OUR FINE STUDENTS ARE EATING THESE FINE MEALS WE COOK...WITH THEIR FINGERS! THE FOOD IS GOING DOWN THEIR THROATS AND UP THEIR NOSES!" *Alma Mater*, Addison Wesley: 2000, p. 202.

begin to make their appearance and can account for between four and six of all courses taken. Students embark upon a major in their third year.

While the Yale-NUS approach has built on the strengths of traditional core curriculum programs, it moves beyond the so-called "Western" tradition by integrating traditions from South and East Asia, as well as the Middle East. Notably, these traditions are not treated in separate cultural area courses, but are addressed in courses that take an explicitly comparative perspective.

The Yale-NUS curriculum was the outcome of a lengthy and intensive planning process that brought together faculty members from a variety of fields. These faculty members viewed themselves both as contributing the gifts of their respective fields and extending themselves beyond those fields to address the general goals of a liberal arts education for our times and our world. To be sure, they had the advantage of getting to create something new, as opposed to revising an already existing curriculum and confronting the various vested interests accreted to it over time. But they nonetheless had to leave some long-standing habits behind. Notably, they had to find it rewarding both to learn about and to teach beyond their own areas of research.[°]

Communicating a passion for one's own field is one of the major attributes of a great teacher. But so is addressing the broader goals of higher education, not to mention sharing the joy of learning itself. And so great teachers need to see themselves not just as members of a department (which is already progress for

---

[°]For additional information, visit www.Yale-NUS.edu/sg. The site includes a lengthy curriculum planning document that is of special interest in terms of how faculty collaborated to shape the program.

those who think of themselves as completely free agents), but as members of the college or university as a whole. In doing so, they strengthen the case for tenure—a case most often made in terms of academic freedom, but which should also be seen as reflecting a deep mutual commitment between a faculty member and an institution, a commitment that truly serves them both.

IV
If I Ran the Zoo

"'But if I ran the zoo'
Said young Gerald McGrew,
'I'd make a few changes,
That's just what I'd do....'"

—Dr. Seuss

"The President is aware of what is going on. That's not to say there is something going on."
    —Ron Ziegler, press secretary to Richard Nixon

Presidents come into their positions with high hopes and serious ambitions. Ideally, those hopes and ambitions are in sync with the mission, strengths, needs, and ongoing well-being of the institutions they will be serving. Presidents soon become aware of the limits on what they are able to accomplish and do well to develop a healthy respect for how much of the institution's vital work is carried out by others. Establishing strong colleague relationships with these others belongs at the top of the agenda.

This is a point well worth emphasizing given current tendencies toward what we might call "leadership fetishism." While leadership is important and good leaders certainly do make a difference, we tend to overemphasize the impact of a chief executive officer and under-emphasize how much of that impact depends upon the ability to motivate, support, and learn from others—in the case of a college or university, those others ranging from faculty to students to staff to fellow administrators to trustees.

This over-valuation of the president's role has fostered out-of-control compensation packages that distance presidents from others laboring in the same institutional vineyard (with the usual exceptions for football coaches and cardiovascular surgeons, in the case of institutions with Division I sports programs and medical schools). It is understandable that trustees from the world of business and finance would look upon the job performed by college presidents and rightly conclude that it compares impressively with the jobs done by presidents of corporations, that it is, in some respects, even more challenging. They thus feel that they must come up with a figure that achieves visibility in their own usual universe of numbers. But these trustees need to be mindful not only of what is most healthy for an academic institution, but also that the salaries of corporate CEOs themselves cannot be explained, much less justified, by any clear measures of productivity and performance.

Most notably, out-sized compensation arrangements drive a wedge between the president and the faculty. This may not be viewed as a problem by trustees who believe that being at odds with the faculty is a clear reflection of a president's leadership abilities. While a president may indeed sometimes have to make hard choices that will distress some significant proportion of the faculty, a truly successful president is able to mobilize support, on an ongoing basis, for decisions that serve the institution's best interests. It is such support that enables decisions to take hold and become consequential in the life of the institution. To put it another way, insofar as faculty are at the core of the particular business that colleges and universities are in, a president's good relationship with the faculty is good for business.

Given the many demands on a president's time and energy, especially at large institutions, it can be difficult to keep those demands from interfering with a core responsibility: ensuring the academic quality of the institution and the education it offers its students. While the immediate duties related to this rest with others, it is the president's job to care enough and know enough to provide the leadership and support required.

Working closely with and through an institution's academic officers, presidents need to see that what is termed "shared governance" is truly shared, as opposed to divided. This involves regular occasions on which administrators and faculty members sit down together to explore a problem and, armed with data, engage in serious discussion. The outcome of such occasions is often quite positive. Moreover, in addition to the manifest function of solving the problem, there is the latent function of building a relationship of mutual respect and trust.

In order for this to occur, faculty members must do their part. This would represent a change in attitude from one often encountered, especially at large universities, in which faculty guard their governance role in the wider institution much the way Fafnir the dragon of Nordic mythology guards its treasure: lying somnolent above it much of the time, but roused to possessive fury when feeling that treasure is threatened.

Given that faculty have a special responsibility when it comes to ensuring the quality of the education offered to students, a more robust involvement in certain ongoing aspects of governance would seem called for. An obvious example would be governance procedures that involve upholding the standards of the academic profession itself. Let me illustrate this point with two situations I experienced in my own years as an administrator.

The first case involved a faculty member highly qualified in her field of specialization, but who seemed to require little if anything from her students. One result was that entire sports teams turned out for her classes—turned out, but not up, since she expected little not only in the way of performance, but also in way of attendance. Though her enrollments were large, she liked to say that she preferred to meet her classes in her office. Somehow the students who enrolled in her classes all received A's. The solution proposed by the provost was, under the circumstances, a relatively modest one: that all of this faculty member's grades be recorded pass/fail, thus stemming the tide of unearned, degraded highest marks. This proposal was taken to the relevant faculty committee whose members concluded, after discussion, that it would be wrong to interfere with a colleague in this manner. The utter fecklessness of this response was exceeded only when the chair of the committee, at a subsequent social occasion, expressed to the provost her wish that the administration would simply "take care of it." One can imagine emergency vehicles from the AAUP turning up, lights flashing, as a response to such administrative action.

In the second case, at a different institution, a once highly distinguished member of the faculty had not been fulfilling her responsibilities appropriately for a number of years, alcoholism playing a part in the situation. As a result, her class enrollments were dwindling to the vanishing point and, even so, her grades were never turned in on time. It had not been possible for members of the academic administration to persuade her to retire; in such situations, special care needs to be taken about matters of age discrimination. It was only when her faculty colleagues on the appointments and tenure committee communicated their readiness to review her case, taking the problems of her professional irresponsibility seriously, that she realized she would be better served by retiring and being granted the title of emeritus professor. The faculty member also realized that there would be no significant financial cost to her, since she had not qualified for merit-based salary increases for many years. In this case, senior faculty members and administrators consulted constructively and collegially to achieve a resolution that was best for the students and respectful of the faculty member's own better days.

The moral of these contrasting stories: in rights begin responsibilities. Those who want to play a strong role in the game of governance need to step up to the plate. Presidents and provosts may always have to make certain unhappy decisions that affect the academic programs of the institution—and it is fair enough that those be the hardest ones—but the more planning and problem-solving that can be done collaboratively, the better.

One key to making shared governance work is an embrace of representative, as opposed to direct, democracy on the part of the faculty. Faculty members must empower and trust their elected representatives to important committees. Only this way is it possible to avoid the frequent fate of well-laid plans: Death by Faculty Meeting.

Another important strategy is to find a clear and interesting way to have faculty members understand the financing of the institution. Well-illustrated presentations by chief financial officers with good communication skills can be quite effective. They are a good way of demonstrating that some of the faculty folklore about how costs could be cut would have minimal, if any, effect on the major cost drivers.

It is also important for faculty members to understand the financial consequences of continuing to add programs without ever subtracting any—the all-too-common approach to the emergence of new scientific and scholarly fields and interests. The negative consequences of addition, as opposed to transformation, are not merely economic, but also curricular as the institution's academic offerings take on the aspect of a zombie movie in which the living co-habit with the undead and anything in between.

Shared governance is also advanced by building a good bridge between faculty and board members, thereby avoiding a situation in which board members view faculty as clueless inhabitants of CloudCuckooLand while faculty members see trustees as extra-terrestrials who appear on the campus planet now and then to wreak havoc. A good way to do this includes bringing faculty members and trustees together in various formal and informal settings. A faculty committee on salaries and benefits has much to learn, for example, by visiting the finance committee of the board. And then there are dinners where trustees can learn more about what faculty members actually do and faculty members can benefit from talking about their work in a way that is clear and interesting to those from very different walks of life.

In promoting a greater shared understanding among various constituencies of the institution, presidents are, in fact, operating not just as chief executive officers, but chief interpretive officers. They must know how to tell the stories that link past and present, connecting an institution's history to where it needs to be heading. At a time of rapid and dislocating change, as is the case for higher education, it can be difficult to do this, but we fail at our peril: the alternative is a total loss of moorings. Presidents who perform this necessary work are thereby also engaging in a central faculty activity: they are teaching.[∞]

In brief and in sum, there is a dimension to the work of a president that deserves more attention than it gets: the responsibility to create and sustain a strong sense of community. Such a sense not only contributes to getting as much necessary work done in as strife-free a way as possible; it is also an end in itself, making members of an academic community look forward to coming to work.

[∞]This aspect of a president's work is reflected well in the felicitously titled *Ever the Teacher* (1988, Princeton University Press), a collection of William Bowen's various writings and speeches during his years as President of Princeton University. Notable among the many personal qualities and professional achievements that account for Bowen's exceptional contributions to higher education are the respect and regard he enjoyed from his faculty colleagues, from his board members, and from students.

V
Community and Communication

"It ain't what I say, it's the way that I say it.
That's all, brother, that's all."

—Mae West

Linguists make a basic distinction between semantics, or the referential properties of language, and pragmatics, aspects of meaning that depend upon and/or define the social context of speech. The major issues that divide us within the academic community belong in the referential content category: issues around tenure, governance, salaries, the curriculum, and general institutional priorities—to name just a few. Given, however, how difficult—not to say seemingly intractable—these issues can be, we might at least not add to the difficulty by how we speak about them.

As for the pragmatic dimensions of speech, another helpful distinction is that between "illocutionary force" and "perlocutionary effect." "Illocutionary force" designates what a speaker intends in a communication. So, for example, if someone says, "How do you do?" this is meant as a general cordial greeting. The expectable and hoped for response would not be, "How do I do what?," nor is it usual for this question to elicit an extended account of the addressee's state of physical and/or mental health. Either reply would constitute a failure of the anticipated perlocutionary effect.

Speakers—for example, college presidents—who believe that the illocutionary force is with them may be intending to communicate compelling information—for example, about the institution's budget or why it is important to have yet another general review of the curriculum. The perlocutionary effect—for example, on faculty members—may, however, be the equivalent of "yada yada yada."

Insofar as administrators and faculty members form separate speech communities, spending an increasing amount of time with their professional peers rather than with one another, communication problems intensify. Administrators, moreover, are likely to have absorbed more of the jargon that continues to proliferate in the professional literature on higher education, jargon that tends to fall on faculty ears somewhere along a range from soporific to maddening. It is however, possible, for presidents, as well as other senior administrators including provosts and chief financial officers, to get important issues across in a way that their audiences find not only informative, but engaging, and even at times entertaining. I have worked with such colleagues and have actually seen it happen.

Problems of communication come to the fore whenever a campus is in a state of crisis. While students are yelling issue-simplifying slogans, presidents may be responding with the prose equivalent of pablum. Faculty members, who have a major role to play in enhancing the light to heat ratio—and, in the best of cases actually play such a role—all too often stay out of the fray. Others undermine their own authority as sources of relative reason and wisdom by behaving like trolls on-line, failing to understand the difference between what one might say in the company of a small group of close friends enjoying adult beverages together and what is appropriate to say in a world of virtual channels of communication in which just about nothing remains private.

Choice of vocabulary is of the essence. Certain hot-button terms cause an immediate and automatic shutdown on the part of some listeners and should thus be used only in the presence of the like-minded. For example, using the term "micro-aggression" to characterize racially insensitive behavior will cause those already blind to common, everyday race-related insults to go on a tear about wimpiness and whining. Hence, a missed opportunity for consciousness raising. The increasingly pervasive term "competencies" is still a turn-off to those who find the term "skills" entirely fitting and proper.

Within the universe of faculty members, the most significant barriers to communication are located along disciplinary, departmental lines. These are borders to be crossed more frequently and effectively if we are to achieve a more intellectually rewarding academic community.

Here, we can take inspiration from an organization that brings together scholars at the very height of their respective fields of research and requires that they communicate with others outside those fields: the

American Philosophical Society (APS). The APS, founded in 1743 by Benjamin Franklin with the help and support of some of his friends (Thomas Jefferson, George Washington, John Marshall, the Marquis de Lafayette....), was, in Franklin's words, intended to "...cultivate the finer arts and improve the common stock of knowledge." As more specialized learned societies emerged over time, the APS remained and remains still a place where scholars and scientists gather for meetings that differ in an edifying way from the conferences they generally attend within their respective fields.

In the course of a single APS meeting, taking April 2014 as an example, one could hear talks on, among other topics: the future of solar energy; warning signs of a looming biodiversity crisis; Woodrow Wilson's political role during World War I; the work of composer Richard Rodgers in his respective collaborations with Lorenz Hart and Oscar Hammerstein. Interestingly, scientists in especially esoteric fields are generally able to make their presentations clear and comprehensible.

To be sure, the APS audience is relatively high-end. And yet, considerable translation effort is involved for successful communication to this audience of widely differing specialists. Well-placed humor also contributes to the success of APS presentations, as it contributes to communication more generally. It would be worth knowing how much and how often the various distinguished members of the APS return to their respective institutions bringing along these same habits to communication with their colleagues in other fields and with their students at various levels of specialization.

There is a growing realization that academics need to extend themselves to wider audiences—both as teachers within their institutions and as contributors to public discourse. Distinguished scholars who are also inspired teachers and good writers have an especially important part to play in these times, as they have at various times in the past. Those who can command a plurality of what linguists call "registers"—forms of speech that are special to particular groups or social settings—can be especially effective. As Nelson Mandela observed, "If you speak to a man in a language he understands it goes to his head. But if you speak to a man in his own language it goes to his heart." Building community is thus not a matter of our all communicating in the same way, but a matter of our caring enough to learn each other's styles.

VI
In Search of *Gemeinschaft*

The German term *Gemeinschaft* has been used in different but related ways, including those well known to sociologists through the work of Ferdinand Tönnies and Max Weber. I use it here, borrowing from both theorists, to designate the experience of community that comes from sharing a common location and certain core values. While colleges and universities should continue to be places where individualism and unforgettable unique personalities can flourish, they certainly stand to benefit from a greater level of community consciousness.

The rewards of *Gemeinschaft* are great, as are the challenges to it—challenges that include the heightened individualism of our society, the changes in information technology that reinforce it, the centrifugal pulls on the higher education curriculum, the growing gulf between faculty members and administrators, the free-agency perspective of faculty members, and the extent to which colleges and universities have felt the need to consider themselves competitors rather than collaborators.

The undergraduate curriculum in our colleges and universities is all too often a barrier to intellectual community. The proliferation of specializations within disciplines and the emergence of interdisciplinary fields have left little room for students to have a common educational experience during their college years. Some institutions have held to a core curriculum throughout this period of growing specialization, a notable example being Columbia University. A number of others that have not wished to follow the path to curricular *Gemeinschaft* quite that far have nonetheless felt a need to make the undergraduate experience more comprehensible, coherent, and meaningful. They have done so by becoming places where faculty members think of themselves not just as a community of scholars but also as a community of teachers, with communal responsibility for shaping the curriculum.

An emphasis on "competencies" over content can also contribute to viewing education in an overly individualized way. If there was once too much of an emphasis on curricular content, there now seems to be too little. While it is important to be clear about what kinds of skills should be expected from a high-quality liberal-arts education, it is important to consider the kind of knowledge that has met the test of time and would give those benefiting from it a common basis for communication and action. We may no longer be able to agree on a particular set of works with which all educated people should be familiar, but that does not absolve us of responsibility for making principled curricular decisions about the kind of material that would be most significant and intellectually challenging.

Achieving a greater level of curricular *Gemeinschaft* requires that faculty members see their individual classes not as private property but as part of a common project that engages them with their colleagues. This may involve rethinking not only what we consider "general education," but major programs as well. It should certainly involve college-wide curricular planning that transcends the interests of one's own department.

All of which means that faculty members discuss matters of teaching as naturally as they discuss matters of research. It also means that all those who serve as academic advisors function as high-quality tour guides for students, pointing out desirable itineraries from arrival to departure and discussing with students what the journey is basically about. On-line tools can also be of help in guiding students through their undergraduate educational experience and are especially useful at larger institutions.

The co-curriculum could similarly benefit from increased coherence. In the current ever-proliferating world of student activities, one sometimes wonders whether the number of student groups will come to equal the number of students. The antidote is for students, as well as the faculty and staff who support them in their activities, to set priorities, to agree together that greater focus would bring greater rewards.

Ongoing changes in information technology present a special challenge to *Gemeinschaft*. As we go about our daily lives, including our campus lives, we are used to seeing people plugged into their respective electronic devices, oblivious to the human beings occupying the same area at the same time. Indeed, we see such behavior even at meetings where people presumably have come together with the express purpose of engaging in some common activity.

In the beginning, however, is a commitment to consider ourselves members of the same community. And here it is interesting to go back to a study published in 1957, in *Administrative Science Quarterly*, by the sociologist Alvin Gouldner, based on research conducted at a liberal arts college in the Midwest. Drawing on the work of Robert K. Merton, Gouldner wished to understand the significance of certain "latent" roles in the social life of the college— that is, roles that were not labeled and formally recognized (as were, for example, "full professor," "assistant professor," "department chair," "president," "dean," etc.), but that nonetheless played a central role in the functioning of the institution.

The latent roles that Gouldner found of particular interest and importance were "cosmopolitans" and "locals." Cosmopolitan faculty members were those whose primary identification was with their professional disciplinary peers wherever these peers might be found; such faculty members would be more than willing to leave their current institution if a better situation awaited them elsewhere in terms of their research interests. Locals, on the other hand, were primarily identified with the institutions in which they found themselves; they tended to be relatively unconnected with ongoing developments in their respective fields. Administrators overwhelmingly fell into the category of locals.

Since that time, faculty members—at least those in the tenured and tenure-track ranks—have become more generally cosmopolitan. Administrators, for their part, have also become more cosmopolitan, developing their own professional associations. The upshot has been a greater distance between faculty and administrators, each belonging to their own worlds, with their own respective concerns and professional jargon. This is a distance that constitutes one of the major obstacles to the health of our colleges and universities.

Surely, the strongest institutions are those whose members are both cosmopolitans and locals. They are cosmopolitans in the breadth of their interests, connections, and sophistication. And yet they are locals as well: bringing all they know and care about to the ongoing vitality of the communities where they live and work.

Envoi

This set of reflections opened on a somber note of the many serious problems facing higher education. Some of these problems are beyond the power of colleges and universities themselves to address, though colleges and universities are all too often held responsible for them. Problems of socio-economic inequality and racial discrimination need to be addressed at a societal level. Solutions to how these deeply entrenched problems play out at colleges and universities will be achieved only through concerted effort over a considerable period of time. They will require ongoing initiatives that enable a wider range of students to succeed at institutions of higher education and that provide achievable and appealing career opportunities for a wider range of potential faculty.

The ongoing financial disinvestment from higher education—public higher education, in partic-ular—on the part of government must be reversed through political action. Colleges and universities need to address their own cost-drivers, needless to say, but this is a formidable challenge, since these include, notably, varsity athletics, with its vigorous and entrenched communities of supporters, and various student life-style amenities, which have come to be seen as entitlements by the very parents who complain about how expensive college has become.

Reducing administrative costs involves its own set of challenges. Some escalating costs result from increasing government regulation. Others are connected with the growing ranks of student-life staff; we are now quite far from a time when students them-selves were responsible for creating their social lives beyond the classroom. Institutions of higher education are also being called upon to provide ever greater levels of clinical support for generations of students who enter college in varying states of stress and distress.

And then there is the proliferation of senior administrative positions—something that colleges and universities may have it more in their power to control. In addition to the growing number of such positions, there are the ever-increasing salaries that go with them. Presidential salaries in particular have reached an inexcusable level as institutions of higher education adopt some of the more unsavory features of the corporate world. We have also seen huge dispar-ities develop within faculty salaries in the context of a competitive star system that has led to some particu-larly costly packages; at the other end, we have seen the rapidly growing proportion of underpaid contin-gent faculty. Both developments threaten the possi-bility of a healthy faculty community.

Then, there are those who believe that the future of higher education lies in the world of on-line programs. The more enthusiastic proponents of this view even claim that, as costs are reduced, quality will be increased. It seems clear, however, that fully on-line programs best serve the teaching and learning of relatively specific skills for relatively specific professional purposes. There are a variety of masters-level programs that are, in fact, the likeliest candidates for MOOC treatment.

In terms of undergraduate education, hybrid approaches that combine on-line resources with actual face-to-face classrooms do indeed show promise. But it is quite likely that the ratio of non-virtual to virtual teaching strategies will replicate the pattern of relative privilege that is already so central to our system of higher education. It will not be the most advantaged members of our society who will see their educations "unbundled" and who will accumulate a set of "badges" in the place of a single undergraduate degree.

In fact, residential colleges and universities have a special role to play in restoring a sense of community to a world where people are losing the ability to be actually, physically together in rewarding ways; a world where people walking down the street apparently talking to themselves are no longer a small number of ambulatory schizophrenics but rather a horde of socially disconnected individuals on cell-phones communicating trivia to distant others.

Faculty who are relatively long-term members of college and university communities include a high proportion of strong-minded individuals who are given to going—and having—their own respective ways. But they also are part of an institution that provides them with various benefits. And they are there for their students whom they will best serve by being there for one another—both as a community of scholars and a community of teachers. ■

Acknowledgments

Some of the material included in "I Do It My Way," "That's Not My Department," and "Culture and Communication" appeared in earlier versions in op ed pieces published in *Inside Higher Education*. "In Search of Gemeinschaft" includes arguments from an essay in *The Chronicle of Higher Education*.

Also available from Prickly Paradigm Press:

continued

continued